HELP!

I'M DEPRESSED

Carol Trahan

Consulting Editor: Dr. Paul Tautges

© 2014 Carol Trahan

ISBN
Paper: 978-1-63342-051-9
ePub: ISBN 978-1-63342-052-6
Kindle: ISBN 978-1-63342-053-3

Shepherd Press
P.O. Box 24
Wapwallopen, PA 18660

www.shepherdpress.com

All Scripture quotations, unless stated otherwise, are from the New King James Version (NKJV) Copyright © 1982 by Thomas Nelson, Inc.

First printed by Day One Publications

Designed by **documen**

Contents

Introduction: "Lord, I'm Drowning in Sorrow"

Troubling thoughts flood my mind. I lie in bed alone, beseeching God on behalf of my three children. The tears spill down my cheeks as I wonder why the Lord seems so far away and why my prayers remain unanswered. Earlier, my daughter had shared what one of her recently married friends posted to another friend on Facebook: "You are going to love marriage." I find myself feeling frustrated, even jealous, as I think about my failed marriage. I remember my wedding day and how excited I was. Never did I imagine my husband would fail morally and end his life after eight short years together.

My thoughts turn to my children and their struggles: to my two daughters, who distrust men and fear marriage, thinking their future husbands might one day be unfaithful to them as well. And then I think about my son, about the bitterness and anguish he has faced and the wrong choices that have deeply scarred his life.

If all this isn't bad enough, I begin the comparison game. Several families come to mind, couples who have strong, happy marriages and children who are doing well. Their success plunges me further into depression. Looking at my own life, I perceive myself as having received an F in both Marriage 101 and Parenting 101. I know I made wrong choices early in my marriage, but later I asked for forgiveness and I have endeavored to walk in obedience to the Lord for many years since. Yet I feel that life has only gone from bad to worse.

Life seems so unfair. Why is it so hard? "Lord, where are you, and why are you not answering my prayers regarding my children?"

At this point I am in the "depths of despair" (as Anne Shirley says in the movie *Anne of Green Gables*). I know I have a choice to make. Am I going to allow these feelings to destroy me or not?

Thankfully, God's Word is deeply embedded in my heart. I know I must choose to meditate on truth, or I will be in deep trouble. The Lord brings several passages to mind:

Great peace have those who love Your law,

And nothing causes them to stumble.
                    (Psalm 119:165)

You will keep him in perfect peace,
Whose mind is stayed on You,
Because he trusts in You.
                    (Isaiah 26:3)

For I know the thoughts that I think
toward you, says the LORD, thoughts of
peace and not of evil, to give you a future
and a hope.
                    (Jeremiah 29:11)

As I meditate on these Scriptures, I recognize that my depression is due to wrong thinking. I have been dwelling on my own reasoning and perception. I have been living with the "But I thought ..." focus. This is the way I *think* things in life should work out, and because they are not going that way, I'm depressed.

By God's grace, I choose to embrace truth and stop dwelling on my foolish understanding. Of course, I'm still hurting (sin always brings heartache), but my focus has changed. I pray to the Lord and express my trust in him. At this point I fall asleep.

I wish I could say that that was my last battle with depression, but such is not the case. This daily struggle has driven me deep into God's Word in search of answers and hope. If you are in the "depths of despair," take heart—you are not alone. Let's walk together through God's Word, and by the end of this journey, may we echo the words of the psalmist:

> Why are you cast down, O my soul?
> And why are you disquieted within me?
> Hope in God;
> For I shall yet praise Him,
> The help of my countenance and my God.
>
> (Psalm 43:5)

1

The Ministry of Sorrow

What would life be like without emotions? Wouldn't it be nice if a switch enabled us to turn our emotions on or off? When things are going well (at least according to our definition of "well"), we could keep the switch on. But when life is falling apart, we could turn the emotion switch off. As a young girl growing up in the 1960s, I remember watching the original *Star Trek*. The character Spock's ability to live by pure logic minus emotions intrigued me. Of course, occasionally the show's writers added a dramatic spin by writing emotion into his character, but for the most part Spock was predictable and logical. Thankfully, God did not make us this way.

Because God made us in his image (Genesis 1:26), emotions are part of his creative work in us. God himself displays a variety of emotions. He is loving, compassionate, and merciful, but he can also be grieved, jealous, and angry (1 John 4:7–8; Psalm 145:8; Genesis 6:6; Nahum 1:2). These emotions, and many more, are part of God's character. Since God is perfect, all emotions within his character are displayed in holiness and perfection. It is hard for us to understand how jealousy or anger can be positive, but that is because we are sinful human beings. Yet for the child of God, emotions serve a vital purpose in God's plan. The challenge we face is learning how to manage them in a way that pleases the Lord.

For the sake of this book, let's consider the emotion of depression, the feeling of deep sadness or sorrow. We can describe the effects of depression in the following ways:

» To make sad or gloomy; lower in spirits; deject; dispirit

» To lower in force, vigor, activity; weaken; make dull

» To lower in amount or value[1]

That definition doesn't sound very positive, does it? In fact, it sounds terrible. How can we make sense of this emotion? Is there any hope, or will this feeling haunt us indefinitely? How can we honor God in the midst of such sadness?

Overwhelmed by Sadness

This feeling of sadness has plagued me often and been particularly debilitating. Many nights I have trouble sleeping. Throughout the day, times of deep discouragement overwhelm my heart. I find myself questioning the Lord, asking why problems seem only to get worse, wondering if circumstances will ever change, and succumbing to the comparison game.

When I began writing this book, I received devastating news about one of my children. I had just completed major surgery and was in the recuperation process, so I was already physically weak. When I heard the news, my emotions plummeted. Many precious sisters in Christ came over to comfort me, to listen, and to lend a helping hand, but the anguish in my heart would not go away. I knew people were praying, and by faith I knew my Lord was in control and working, but the news hurt so deeply. How could anything that hurt so much ever turn out for good? This makes no sense whatsoever, I thought. My youngest daughter asked me if I was doing all right. I looked at her and said, "No."

I know this feeling well as a widow. When my husband, Jeff, confessed to immorality and later took his life, the emotional pain was beyond description. Shortly after Jeff's death, I was with my parents for the holidays. My father, a World War II veteran, often watched war movies, and one evening we watched *Sink the Bismarck!* In the movie the director of operations was considered a very cold person, but as the plot unfolded I began to understand why this man was so hardened. His wife had been killed in a bombing raid, and he had just received the news that his son was missing. As he spoke to the officer assisting him, he said, "When my wife was killed, I never thought it was possible to feel such pain. I decided then and there that I would never become emotionally attached to a person again." This man's coldness was his defense. He'd hurt so deeply for so long that his answer (albeit a wrong one) was to fence himself off from people and emotions. But his attempt to handle the depression his way brought about only greater pain.

If we are God's children we cannot try to handle our pain in this manner. We cannot become hardened or cold toward God or others. Such a response is an easy trap to fall into because instinctively we don't want to hurt, and in our minds that desire often translates into keeping people at a distance. But that is selfish. God would rather that we surrender to his purpose through the sorrow so we can help others in the midst of their pain.

Perplexed but Not in Despair

As I slumped on my couch, still cringing from the news about my child, the Lord reminded me of his faithfulness. Had I forgotten God's mighty works these past seventeen years? He had continually provided for me and my children and answered countless prayers. He had shown his tender care over and over, and now I was once again questioning his love and goodness. How could my faith be so weak? Hadn't I learned anything over the years?

The Lord brought to my mind 2 Corinthians 4, one of my favorite chapters of Scripture. Twice this passage exhorts us not to lose heart (vv. 1, 16), and my eyes were drawn to verses 8–11:

> We are hard-pressed on every side, yet
> not crushed; we are perplexed, but not
> in despair; persecuted, but not forsaken;
> struck down, but not destroyed—always
> carrying about in the body the dying of
> the Lord Jesus, that the life of Jesus also

> may be manifested in our body. For we
> who live are always delivered to death for
> Jesus' sake, that the life of Jesus also may
> be manifested in our mortal flesh.

These verses encouraged my heart. I was truly perplexed and deeply saddened by the news, but I did not need to despair. This was another opportunity for God to manifest the life of Jesus in and through my life. God was teaching me the ministry of sorrow, a ministry of helping the hurting through the comfort I receive from the Lord Jesus Christ.

Why So Much Sorrow?

It may surprise you to count how many Bible characters experienced times of deep discouragement and sadness. Jeremiah wanted to quit (Jeremiah 20:7–9), Elijah wanted to die (1 Kings 19:4), Job wished he had died at birth (Job 3:11), Moses thought God had placed too great a burden on him and requested that God kill him (Numbers 11:14–15), David and his men wept as Absalom pursued them (2 Samuel 15:23, 30), Hannah was in bitterness of soul (1 Samuel 1:10, 15), Peter wept bitterly after denying the Lord (Luke 22:62), and Paul despaired even of life (2 Corinthians 1:8).

How does discouragement affect us? Looking at Scripture, we can identify several symptoms of those who were discouraged. They experienced a loss of appetite, wept much, and felt abandoned by God (Psalm 42:3; 77:7–9). They were overwhelmed and felt trapped, heavily oppressed, and trampled (Psalm 66:11–12). At times it seemed as if they were drowning in their sorrow (Psalm 42:7). They also went through periods of insomnia, the inability to speak (Psalm 77:4), loss of hope, and the desire to quit or even die (1 Kings 19:4; Lamentations 3:18).

Heartache Is Everywhere

This picture may look pretty bleak. Why is there so much sorrow? The answer lies in the fall of man. God's original perfect creation lacked sorrow. All that God made was very good (Genesis 1:31). Yet Adam and Eve chose to disobey God, bringing sin, disease, death, and heartache into the world. All of creation was cursed, and we experience the resulting sorrow.

> *Through one man sin entered the world,*
> *and death through sin, and thus death*
> *spread to all men because all sinned.*
> (Romans 5:12)

All of us are sinners, and wherever there is sin, devastation and sorrow follow.

Looking at the world today, we can see the effects of sin everywhere. The Bible describes sinful people as, for example, sexually immoral, wicked, covetous, malicious, envious, murderous, full of strife and deceit, haters of God, violent, proud, disobedient to parents, untrustworthy, unloving, unforgiving, unmerciful, lacking self-control, brutal, and lovers of money, pleasure, and themselves (Romans 1:29–31; 1 Timothy 3:2–4).

Wow, talk about sorrow! This is the result of all of us choosing to live our lives in defiance of God. Created as dependent creatures to love and worship our Creator, we have chosen to rebel and pursue our own agendas. You may argue that these characteristics do not describe what you are really like. Yet the Scriptures teach that no one is righteous and that all of us have gone astray (Romans 3:10–12). We are all guilty of loving ourselves and following our own way.

As sinners we are all separated from God. Our sin requires a penalty, which is death—eternal separation from God in the lake of fire (Romans 5:8, 12; 6:23). At this point you might be wondering how we can be saved from this penalty. Thankfully, God has not left us to ourselves. The gospel (good news) is that along with the curse came God's promise of a redeemer (Genesis 3:15). In God's perfect time, he would send his Son into the world to redeem us from this curse so that we could be adopted into his family (Galatians 4:4–5; Luke 19:10). This Son was the Lord Jesus Christ, who died for our sins, was buried, and rose again. Salvation from the penalty of our sin is available only through him (1 Corinthians 15:1–4; John 14:6). We can be saved through repentance (turning from sin) and faith in Jesus (turning to God) by putting our trust in Jesus Christ alone, thus believing the gospel (Acts 20:21; Ephesians 1:13–14). Those who are saved become children of God, having been delivered from the power of darkness and transferred into the kingdom of the Lord Jesus Christ (Colossians 1:13).

For God's children, heaven is our home, and in that day when we are with the Lord, we will experience no more sorrow (Revelation 21:3–4). All creation waits and even groans, much like a woman in labor, for the day when it will be delivered from the bondage of corruption (Romans 8:19–23). Until that time of deliverance, we live in this fallen world and experience varying degrees of sorrow, but there is a purpose—conformity to Christ. We are called to be like Jesus. He was

> despised and rejected by men,
> A Man of sorrows and acquainted
>   with grief.
>
> (Isaiah 53:3)

When I consider that Jesus humbled himself and became obedient to the death of the cross (Philippians 2:8), my own sorrows pale in comparison. Understanding God's purpose helps me to look at my discouraging circumstances and times of depression from a different perspective.

The Puzzle of Depression

Why are we depressed? At this point let me say that I am dealing with depression from a biblical perspective, not from a medical one. Though medically related causes of depression do exist—health abnormalities that are truly measurable by medical professionals—I am a biblical counselor, not a physician.[2] Some would argue that their depression is "biochemical" in nature. Addressing the issue of chemical imbalances is beyond the scope of this book. Whether someone should take drugs for the treatment of depression is a decision he or she should make with a physician. For the Christian, however, the priority is to walk with the Lord in humility and dependence and to seek his will above all else.

Asking yourself the following three questions may be helpful:

» Do I want God's best?

» Am I committed to obeying the Lord in all he reveals to me?

» Which am I more concerned about: God's glory and purpose, or relief from my sorrow or difficulty?

These questions will help you ascertain what your real goal is. Although medication may serve a purpose and bring relief, we must ask ourselves whether it will address the root issue. We don't want to short-circuit the lessons God wants us to learn, even if they hurt. Many of our greatest lessons will come through the school of sorrow.

Let's return to the question "Why are we depressed?" As I awoke the morning of writing this chapter, my heart was filled with sadness. My daughter wanted to talk with me, but I wasn't interested. I was scheduled to speak to a group of ladies at 9:00 a.m. on the topic of discouragement. "Oh brother," I thought. "How am I going to do this?" I didn't feel like talking to anyone, and I certainly didn't want to go and speak to a group of ladies. I simply wanted to wallow in my sorrow.

Why was I depressed? This day (June 7) would

have been my twenty-fifth wedding anniversary, but all I could think of were the many years of loneliness, heartache, and struggle. Feeling like a total failure, I was deeply discouraged. This wasn't the way life was supposed to be. The night before, I had looked at my wedding pictures. Never did I imagine that the script of my life would play out the way it has. Life wasn't going the way I thought it should.

Solving the depression puzzle is complex; however, much of the sadness we experience is due to difficulty that comes into our lives— difficulty we have no control over. We react to circumstances because they interrupt our agendas, peace, and security. We then interpret the difficulty in one of two ways: based on our own understanding or according to Scripture. In truth, our view of God is the most important thing about us. A. W. Tozer says, "Nothing twists and deforms the soul more than a low or unworthy conception of God."[3] Putting the pieces together as to why we are depressed is directly related to our view of God. If we have a low view of God, we will interpret difficulty based on our own understanding. But if our view of God is exalted, we will look at difficulty through the lens of Scripture.

How Is *Your* View of God?

Our thinking directly affects our feelings and subsequent actions. If our view of God is not based on truth as revealed in the Scriptures, wrong feelings and actions will follow.

Let's take my example above. Viewing my difficulty from my own understanding made me miserable. It seemed as if God had abandoned me, and life was unfair. It made no sense that my marriage had failed or that my children had these scars. I'd been praying for years that God would heal my children, but nothing seemed to be happening. The result of this thinking led to depression. What actions were the result? I didn't want to talk to anyone or go to work; I simply wanted to retreat to my room and sulk. I didn't want others to be blessed. I wanted them to hurt as I was hurting. I was miserable, and I wanted everyone else to be miserable too.

What was going on in my heart?

» Wrong thinking: I viewed the circumstances based on my own understanding; therefore, in my view, God was neither good nor fair

» Wrong feelings: depression

» Wrong actions: isolation, harsh words, irresponsibility

You can see the progression, which leads only to greater sorrow.

In another book in this series, *Help! I'm A Single Mom*, I point out that in every circumstance there are two stories going on. Since I have already covered the concept there, let me summarize. The "mini-story" is the problem I am experiencing, which dominates my thoughts and plummets me into depression. The "big story" is the plan of God. He is in control of this circumstance. How does he want me to respond so others can see a living Redeemer?

There are also two wars going on. The "agenda war" occurs because this circumstance has interrupted my life and the plans I had. The "glory war" rages between what I want and God's glory. This circumstance has been divinely prepared or permitted by God for his glory.

In this case, the mini-story is my depression; this circumstance has interrupted the agenda I have for my life and I want it fixed. Now!

A war rages between God's glory and my agenda. If I do not choose to humble myself and surrender to God's plan, I will persist in trying to "fix" the problem or "manipulate" the Lord (a notion that is utter foolishness) until I get my way. Since this is a war I cannot win (thankfully), I will wallow in my depression and in the process make others miserable. This may seem harsh, but if we are honest, this is often the way we choose to function.

At this point you might ask whether all depression is due to wrong thinking. Let's go back to the definition of depression—"to make sad or lower in spirits"—and the question "Why are we depressed?" Do we have legitimate reasons to be sad? I believe the answer is "yes." Living in a fallen world where sin abounds, we will experience sadness. I'm sure you can identify many situations or people who have brought grief to your heart; however, I believe we need to make a distinction between the sadness we feel as a result of painful circumstances and how we choose to respond to sorrow.

Depression Is a Choice

Living in a state of depression is a choice. A circumstance may make you sad or lower your spirits, but it does not mean you must live in depression. If you fail to see God's purpose in the difficulty, the result will be depression and the loss of hope. Remember, God's goal is conformity to Christ. This means our passion must always be to do those things that please our heavenly Father (John 8:29). Did the Lord Jesus Christ experience sorrow? Indeed he did. But he saw beyond the sorrow to his Father's redemptive plan; therefore, he endured the cross for the joy that was set before him (Hebrews 12:2). As we choose to focus on the Lord and embrace his purpose, our sorrows take on new meaning.

One of my favorite devotionals is *Streams in the Desert*. Consider the following:

> *To have a sympathizing God we must have a suffering Savior, and there is no true fellow-feeling with another save in the heart of him who has been afflicted like him.*
>
> *We cannot do good to others save at a cost to ourselves, and our afflictions are the price we pay for our ability to sympathize. He who would be a helper must first be a sufferer.*
>
> *The most comforting of David's psalms were pressed out by suffering; and if Paul had not had his thorn in the flesh we had missed much of that tenderness which*

> *quivers in so many of his letters.*
>
> *The present circumstance, which presses so hard against you (if surrendered to Christ), is the best-shaped tool in the Father's hand to chisel you for eternity. Trust Him, then. Do not push away the instrument lest you lose the work. The school of suffering graduates rare scholars.*[4]

Offenses will come. We will receive distressing news, and sometimes we will feel overwhelmed. Jesus told us we would experience tribulation in this world (John 16:33). There isn't a day that goes by that I don't feel sadness when I look at my children growing up without their father. I meet hurting people everywhere. Listening to the evening news on TV (or via the Internet) is enough to discourage anyone. This, however, does not mean we must live in a state of continual depression.

Hannah, for example, felt great sorrow due to her barrenness and the provocation of Peninnah (1 Samuel 1:5–7). Asaph sorrowed when he looked at the seeming prosperity of the wicked (Psalm 73) and experienced deep depression when he thought that God had abandoned him (Psalm 77).

The apostle Paul tells us that he had "great sorrow and continual grief in [his] heart" due to the lost condition of his kinsmen (Romans 9:2). Did these individuals experience sorrow? Clearly the answer is "yes." How did they handle their sorrow? How would God have *us* handle the sadness we have experienced? We will address these questions in the next chapter.

Our Response to Sorrow

When God created Adam and placed him in the garden of Eden, he gave him this command: "Of every tree of the garden you may freely eat; but of the tree of the knowledge of good and evil you shall not eat, for in the day that you eat of it you shall surely die" (Genesis 2:16–17).

God gave Adam the freedom to choose. Adam could enjoy the bounty of all God had provided, or he could choose to disobey, the result of which would be death. God later created Eve and brought her to Adam. Scripture does not tell us whether God communicated the same command directly to Eve, but we can infer that her husband communicated it to her. Since Adam and Eve were perfect and sinless, they had no desire to disobey. Therefore, temptation must have come from without, and Genesis 3 introduces us to the serpent (Satan).

What is the enemy's goal? Scripture teaches us that he has come to steal, destroy, and kill (John 10:10). He wants to devour our faith and incite doubt about God's character (1 Peter 5:8). Satan approached Eve and tried to destroy her confidence in the goodness of God; he wanted her to doubt God, to question his provision. The enemy is crafty and a master at deception. He drew Eve's attention away from all she had (every tree of the garden) and toward the one forbidden thing.

You might wonder why God gave the command not to eat of this particular tree. It is clear that God gave mankind a choice. However, we know God's character from Scripture. When he says "no," his prohibition is always best and for our protection and good. God was not "holding out" on Adam and Eve; his command not to eat of this tree was out of love for his created beings.

We Are a Product of Our Choices

Sadly, Eve succumbed to the temptation. She took the fruit and ate it (Genesis 3:6). She made her choice; she believed the enemy's lie and disobeyed God. Now Adam had a choice to make as his wife handed the fruit to him. Would he obey God? He faced a major dilemma. If he obeyed God, he would be separated from his wife, for she had now experienced spiritual death and would eventually suffer physical death. Adam made his choice: he took the fruit and ate it. As a result, he too experienced spiritual death and would also die physically.

What did Adam and Eve do? They chose to follow what God had created rather than their Creator. Eve chose to follow the serpent, and Adam followed his wife. They

> exchanged the truth of God for the lie, and worshiped and served the creature rather than the Creator, who is blessed forever.
>
> (Romans 1:25)

Why was this decision so significant? I want us to understand that we are products of our choices. Circumstances and people do not determine our destiny. Rather, our responses to circumstances and people determine whom we will become.

Let's go back to my depression scenario. Is it legitimate and appropriate to feel sad because of difficult circumstances (loss, pain, abuse, and so forth)? Of course it is. Does this mean we should live as depressed people? The answer is a resounding "no"!

The Anguish of Barrenness

Let's look at Hannah, who faced a heartbreaking scenario. Her husband, Elkanah, dearly loved her, but she could not have children (1 Samuel 1:2). John MacArthur says, "Childlessness carried a reproach in a culture where blessings were tied to birthrights and family lines."[5] To add to her anguish, Elkanah's second wife, Peninnah, *could* have children. As if barrenness weren't enough to deal with (Proverbs 30:15–16), Peninnah was a rival who continually provoked Hannah to make her miserable.

Put yourself in Hannah's place. Not only must you share your husband with another woman, one who can give him children while you cannot—but also this other woman takes every opportunity to remind you of your barrenness. This taunting was not a one-time occurrence; it happened on a continual basis. How did Hannah feel as a result of her barrenness and Peninnah's provocation? Scripture tells us that she was "in bitterness of soul"; she did not eat and wept in anguish (1 Samuel 1:7, 10).

Knowing that her heart was grieved, Elkanah asked Hannah four questions (1:8), but she did not answer her husband. This woman experienced deep mental pain, but how did she handle her depression? She went directly to the Lord in prayer (1:10–11), pouring out her soul in honesty. Eli, the priest, misunderstood her and accused her of drunkenness, but she did not lash out; rather, she shared her situation honestly with him. When she left her burden with the Lord, her depression was gone (1:18; also see Psalm 55:22; 1 Peter 5:7).

Hannah chose to trust in God's wisdom and care. Why was she able to do so? Because she had a right view of God. She knew that he alone was holy and worthy of her trust. He was her rock, and she recognized that he had all knowledge and would judge righteously. She rejoiced in the Lord and extolled the greatness of her God (2:1–10). Was Hannah's request granted? Yes, but not right away. According to the text, as she and her husband arose early in the morning to worship the Lord, God remembered her, but she did not conceive immediately (1:19–20): "it came to pass *in the process of time* that Hannah conceived and bore a son" (v. 20, emphasis mine).

Hannah's choice to trust God led to a heart of worship, submission, and joy even before her request was granted. Although circumstances had brought her sadness, she did not live in a state of depression. Do you think this situation was easy for her? I doubt it, but she still made the choice to believe and obey the Lord.

Comparison Kills Contentment

In Psalm 73, Asaph shared from his heart what many of us as God's people feel but are afraid to say. He was deeply discouraged as he pondered the seeming prosperity of the wicked while the righteous experienced trouble. He knew that God is good to his people ("Israel," v. 1). He understood that God blesses the pure in heart (see Matthew 5:8), but in his own life he was perplexed by the many difficulties he faced. He was stumbling and ready to fall (Psalm 73:2–3) as his thoughts were filled with envy.

Reasoning from his own understanding and wallowing in self-pity, he believed that God was unfair. The ungodly were not in trouble or pain; they were not plagued but were full of pride and violence. They had everything they could want and had no compassion. They mocked God, yet were still at ease and prosperous (vv. 3–12). He then argued the futility of walking in righteousness: "Surely I have cleansed my heart in vain, and washed my hands in innocence" (v. 13). This is a stinging accusation. He was saying that living a righteous life was empty, futile. He saw no benefit in having a pure heart since the wicked seemed to prosper while he only suffered. At the beginning of the psalm, he had acknowledged that God was good to the pure in heart, but somehow he thought he was the exception.

Why did he feel this way? From his perspective, his life was one of unending affliction and discipline (v. 14), and he was afraid to say anything, believing this would betray his people (v. 15). As he continued to think upon these things, he plunged into deeper depression (v. 16).

Perhaps his words describe how you feel. As you look at the lives of others in comparison with your own, maybe you become deeply discouraged. From your perspective, others are blessed, but you are suffering. This attitude leads only to deeper depression because comparison kills contentment. Choosing to dwell on what we *don't* understand and comparing ourselves with others will yield the fruit of discontentment and misery.

Let's look at the rest of the psalm. Did Asaph remain in this state of depression? Thankfully, he did not. But how did he resolve his dilemma? His focus changed as he entered the sanctuary (holy place) of God. Instead of dwelling in self-pity and trying to figure things out from his finite understanding, he turned his focus toward the Lord (v. 17). Now he understood the end of the ungodly, which is destruction. He described this "end" in verses 18–19:

> Surely You set them in slippery places;
> You cast them down to destruction.
> Oh, how they are brought to desolation, as
>   in a moment!
> They are utterly consumed with terrors.

What a change of perspective! He realized that although the ungodly might have great prosperity now, this was the best it would ever be. Once they died, their lives would be "consumed with terrors" for eternity.

The realization of how he had accused God of being unfair broke his heart. He recognized the folly of his former thinking and compared himself to an animal (vv. 21–22). What happened to cause such a drastic change in Asaph's heart? He spent time in the presence of God, and as a result he knew that God was sovereign, holy, and perfect in all his doings. Asaph was not alone in this recognition.

Job also struggled greatly with his suffering.

Over time he accused God of not answering and even being cruel (Job 30:19–28). Of course, when we consider what Job experienced, who wouldn't struggle? When God confronted him with his accusations, he told Job that his darkening counsel was the product of words without knowledge (38:2). When we, as finite human beings, try to figure out the infinite mind of God and why the Lord works as he does, we "darken" (confuse) counsel because we speak without knowledge. The next four chapters of Job (38–41) give us a glimpse into the greatness of God's majesty and power.

How did Job respond after being in God's presence? He recognized that he was vile and couldn't answer; he placed his hand over his mouth and did not speak (40:3–5). Job further realized that God can do anything he pleases and that no one can thwart God's purpose. In foolishness he had spoken without understanding. He then repented in dust and ashes (42:2–6).

Let's return to Psalm 73. Asaph was no longer in depression; quite the opposite. He recognized that God was continually with him and held him by his right hand. In other words, the Lord would support him and hold him straight; God would guide him and then receive him into glory. This thought reminds me of Jude 24:

> Now to Him who is able to keep you
>   from stumbling,
> And to present you faultless
> Before the presence of His glory with
>   exceeding joy ...

All Asaph ever needed, both in heaven and on earth, was the Lord. Though his flesh and heart would fail, God was his strength and portion forever (Psalm 73:23–26).

Asaph concluded this psalm by stating that the ungodly would be destroyed. He would draw near to the Lord and trust him (vv. 27–28). This is the choice we must make. When life makes no sense, we cannot play the comparison game or try to figure everything out. The result will be depression. Instead, we must humble ourselves in the presence of God, see with the eyes of faith, and trust the Lord with all our hearts (Proverbs 3:5–6).

Lord, Where Are Your Mercies?

Asaph gives us further insight into the cure for depression in Psalm 77. In Psalm 73, he was depressed because of his perception that God was unfair. In Psalm 77, he agonizes over whether God has abandoned him. As we look at this psalm, we see that Asaph was definitely in the "depths of despair" as he thought upon the Lord.

He begins with hope and anchors the reader to the truth that God does hear us when we cry out to him (v. 1). As we proceed, the words of Asaph draw us into his anguish. He was in deep distress but refrains from telling us the cause. This exclusion is helpful because any type of heartache we experience will fit his description. He couldn't find comfort, and the more he thought upon the Lord, the more troubled he became. He moaned and felt overwhelmed. He couldn't sleep and even accused God of holding his eyes open. He couldn't even speak. He remembered happier days, which only augmented his depression, and diligently sought an answer to his despair (vv. 2–6).

At this point he asks several heart-wrenching questions pertaining to God's character (vv. 7–9). Asaph is completely transparent here. His anguish had led him to the point of desperation, even hopelessness. He wanted an answer from the Lord. In modern-day vernacular, he definitely fit the bill of someone clinically depressed.

Remembering God's Works and Wonders

Asaph was once again faced with a choice. He could succumb to his depression and hopelessness or shift his focus. What did he do? Let's consider the steps he took.

» He didn't deny his anguish (v. 10). We too go through painful circumstances that bring us sorrow. It is of no benefit to deny the pain or claim it isn't really there. We hurt, but this pain has a purpose. If we embrace God's agenda, he will use the pain for his glory, our good, and the good of others.

» He remembered past times when God showed himself to be mighty (v. 10). The "right hand" of the Lord often speaks of God's power. Asaph remembered times when God's power and strength were evident in his life.

» He remembered the Lord's works and wonders of old (v. 11). He chose to think on God's works not only in the present, but also in the many wonders God did in the past (see Psalms 78:7; 111:2–4, 7).

» He not only remembered but also meditated (pondered or dwelled) on God's works. Then he chose to talk of them (v. 12).

» According to verse 12, God did exactly what he said he would do. From verse 13 to the end of the chapter, Asaph talks of God's marvelous character and deeds. It might be helpful for you to read these verses at this time.

What a contrast from the beginning of the chapter! Was Asaph depressed anymore? Certainly not! Had his circumstances changed? I don't believe so. What *did* change was his focus. Notice that he said "I will" several times, and then he followed through by extolling the character of God. Again we see the importance of engaging our wills.

One summer I had the privilege of speaking to a group of young ladies at a Christian camp. My co-speaker, who was ministering in the general sessions, shared the message "Your Attitude Is Your Choice." We choose whether we want to live in a state of depression. When she lived at home, my eldest daughter posted this saying on her bathroom mirror: "Life is 10% of what happens to you and 90% of what you make it."

From Accusation to Adoration

Psalm 13 gives another apt description of depression and how it is resolved. We can see a progression through this psalm. David went from despair and accusation (vv. 1–2) to request and prayer (vv. 3–4), and finally to restored worship and adoration (vv. 5–6). Let's break the psalm down a bit more.

What happened in verses 1–2? David was deeply depressed and asked four "How long?" questions, accusing God of forgetting him and hiding his face. In the Old Testament, the face of God was associated with blessing. In his effort to try to figure out why he was experiencing such distress, David came up empty. He believed the enemy was prevailing and his sorrow was unending. For David, the temporary had become permanent. He felt abandoned; his thoughts were dark and his feelings were out of control.

Beginning in verse 3 and continuing in verse 4, David begged God to hear him. He no longer accused the Lord but pleaded (supplicated) before God. He asked God to illumine his understanding; in other words, David needed wisdom. He gives us a powerful example, one reiterated in the New Testament. Paul prayed this same prayer for the Ephesians (Ephesians 1:17–18), and James encouraged God's children to ask for wisdom when they were going through trials (James 1:2–8). David knew that if God did not intervene, he would not survive, and the enemy would gain the upper hand. David was concerned about God's reputation. We see a progression here: David went from despair and accusation to prayer.

Verses 5–6 demonstrate an amazing transition. David made a choice; he engaged his will. "But I have trusted ... My heart shall rejoice ... I will sing." What happened to David? Did his circumstances change? Not that we can see; however, David changed his thinking. In verses 1–2, his view of God was unworthy and skewed; his thinking was based on circumstances and his own understanding. David must have known his attitude was clearly wrong because he didn't stay in despair. He proceeded to prayer and refocused on the Lord. He knew that God answered prayer, and he was concerned about how others would perceive his God if the enemy triumphed. David clearly had a reputation for being a man after God's own heart.

As a result of prayer, God transformed David's thinking. His view of God was back where it belonged. He knew his God was merciful and that the Lord was his Savior. He also knew that God was good and had dealt bountifully with him. His right thinking led to right feelings (joy expressed in song) and right actions (trust and speaking truth). David had gone from accusation to adoration.

What about you? Is this same transition possible? I believe it is, although it is not easy. We can go from despair to trust as we choose to pray and refocus. We must ask the same questions as the psalmist in Psalms 42–43 and come to the same conclusions. Three times he asked, "Why are you cast down [depressed], O my soul? And why are you disquieted within me?" (42:5, 11; 43:5). What was his answer? He counseled himself (and all of us who read the Scriptures) to hope in God and choose to praise him. Why must we respond this way? Because God is the help or salvation of our countenances, and he is our God. What more do we need?

A few years ago, Pastor Mike Summers of Countryside Baptist Church, Olathe, Kansas, said, "If you have God, you have everything, and if you have everything, you have need of nothing." Pastor Summers is exactly right. The Lord is our God, and he is enough!

Our Hope in Sorrow

"Therefore, having been justified by faith, we have peace with God through our Lord Jesus Christ, through whom also we have access by faith into this grace in which we stand, and rejoice in hope of the glory of God. And not only that, but we also glory in tribulations, knowing that tribulation produces perseverance; and perseverance, character; and character, hope. Now hope does not disappoint, because the love of God has been poured out in our hearts by the Holy Spirit who was given to us" (Romans 5:1–5). These precious verses reveal the importance of hope in our lives. Without hope, we have no desire to continue; we lose the will to go on.

The one who lives in a continual state of depression is in great danger of losing hope. In some cases, depressed people have lost all hope, and tragically some even choose to end their lives. I watched my husband go from depression, due to his sinful choices, to despair and ultimately to suicide. The scars left by his choice run very deep both in my children and in me. But I have chosen not to succumb to depression and hopelessness because I know those are clearly not what God wants for his children.

Jesus understood the devastation sorrow can bring to our hearts. As he prepared his disciples for his coming death, he knew that sorrow could overwhelm them. Therefore, he encouraged them by pointing them through the sorrow to the hope they had in him. Although his disciples would sorrow, their sorrow would be turned to joy because they would see Jesus again (John 16:5–6, 20–22). Sadness or sorrow is a powerful emotion that can overwhelm us. This is why it is so important that we understand our hope, so that we are not "swallowed up with too much sorrow" (2 Corinthians 2:7).

Lessons from Mary Magdalene

After Jesus was crucified, Mary Magdalene stood outside the tomb weeping. Jesus had transformed her life, and from the time of her conversion she had ministered to her Lord and had not wanted to be parted from him (Luke 8:1–2). Now, as she stood by the tomb, all seemed hopeless.

When she looked into the tomb, two angels

asked her why she was weeping (John 20:11–13). As I read this, I am surprised. Usually the appearance of angels brings fear to the one beholding them. It is possible that they appeared as men and that she recognized them only as such (although we cannot know for sure). Her mind was preoccupied with two facts: someone had taken away her Lord, and she did not know where he had been laid. Sorrow had consumed this woman.

She later turned and saw Jesus, although she did not recognize him. The text does not tell us why she did not recognize the Lord, but several possible explanations are worth considering. Perhaps tears blurred her vision, or maybe it was still so dark that she was unable to see him clearly. It is also possible that God withheld her eyes from beholding him, much as he did with the disciples on the road to Emmaus. More likely, I believe, is the fact that the last time she saw the Lord, he was a broken, bruised, and bloody spectacle as a result of the Roman brutality inflicted on him. Now, after his resurrection, he still had the nail-scarred hands and side, but his glorified body was no longer beaten and battered.

Jesus asked her why she was weeping. Her mind was still preoccupied with the fact that someone had taken away her Lord; she wanted to know where he was. But when Jesus called her by name, she immediately knew he was her Lord.

What happened to Mary? Her sorrow turned to joy as soon as she recognized her Master's voice calling her name. Why was this so? Jesus said,

> My sheep hear My voice, and I know
> them, and they follow me. And I give
> them eternal life, and they shall never
> perish; neither shall anyone snatch them
> out of My hand.
>
> (John 10:27–28; also see 10:3–4)

The realization that Jesus was no longer dead but alive and that he had not abandoned her brought hope to Mary's broken heart.

What is our hope in sorrow? We serve a living, risen Savior who has conquered death and "brought life and immortality to light through the gospel" (2 Timothy 1:10). The Scriptures give us hope from Genesis to Revelation. Yes, we are sinners, and this sin has brought great sorrow. But the gospel changes everything. God has commanded the light to shine out of darkness through his gospel (2 Corinthians 4:6). The apostle Paul tells us in 2 Corinthians 4:15–18 that all things (and *all* means *all)* are for our sakes.

God's grace is abundant, and "our light affliction ... is working for us a far more exceeding and eternal weight of glory." Because of this, we must not lose heart but keep our eyes on what is unseen (the eternal) rather than on what is seen (the physical).

Two Travel Partners: Suffering and Glory

Years ago, Dr. Les Ollila, chancellor of Northland International University, described suffering and glory as two travel partners. Wherever we see suffering in a person's life—to which he or she responds with humility, submission, and obedience—glory will follow. Scripture clearly teaches this truth:

> For I consider that the sufferings of
> this present time are not worthy to be
> compared with the glory which shall be
> revealed in us.
>
> (Romans 8:18)

As we conclude this chapter, let me give five exhortations based on truths from Romans 8:16–39 that have enabled me to experience hope and great joy in the midst of sorrow.

» Embrace the hope you have in God (vv. 16–17, 24–25). We are God's adopted children and joint heirs with Christ. This, of course, is true only for the children of God who have believed the gospel. As God's children, we have this hope that cannot disappoint us.

» Embrace the Spirit's intercession (vv. 26–27). This has been a precious promise to me. How often I have been overwhelmed and have felt as if I could not pray. Knowing at those times that God's Spirit was interceding for me has made all the difference. The Spirit of God is our Comforter/Helper, who will neither leave us nor forsake us (John 14:16).

» Embrace God's promise that all will work together for good (v. 28). We know this truth, but do we really believe it? This promise fits with the next truth.

» Embrace God's purpose (v. 29). The promise "All things work together" is for those who love the Lord and are called according to his purpose. What is this purpose? It is not our happiness, ease, or agenda; it is conformity to Christ. The sorrow we experience should not be wasted. God means it to make us more like Jesus. By the way, what God starts, he finishes.

All those whom God predestined and called will be glorified.

»   Embrace God's love (vv. 31–39). Nothing can separate us from the love of God for us. This should bring forth heartfelt thankfulness. Calvary love sent the Lord Jesus to die for vile sinners. This is amazing love! This kind of love leaves no room for self-pity.

How wonderful is the hope God has given us in the midst of sorrow! How are you doing? Remember, living in a state of depression is a choice. Considering our hope in God, why should we choose to live in depression? May we be able to say with Paul,

> I am filled with comfort. I am exceedingly joyful in all [my] tribulation.
>
> (2 Corinthians 7:4)

CONCLUSION:
GOD, MY EXCEEDING JOY

I often take long walks in the morning, weather permitting. The few days before writing this I especially enjoyed my walks. The weather was perfect and the scenery gorgeous. The north woods of Wisconsin where I was living can be especially beautiful during the late spring and early summer. I used the walks not only to clear my head but also to extend praise and prayer to the Lord. As I walked and talked to the Lord, my heart was filled with mixed emotions. Soon I would be moving to the island of Guam, where I would have the privilege of serving with Harvest Ministries. Although I was very excited, I also experienced much sorrow as I left a ministry that had so greatly impacted my life.

For almost twenty years I was part of Northland Baptist Bible College (now known as Northland

International University). It was to this very special place that my husband and I came to train for ministry twenty-two years ago. God greatly used the people there, specifically Dr. Les Ollila and Marty and Tami Herron, to impact my life. I was a discontented, bitter woman when I came. Through the philosophy of "life touching life" and the preaching on brokenness and revival, God has since transformed my life.

During the two years Jeff and I were at Northland together (1989–1991), I heard these principles taught and watched the faculty and staff flesh them out in their lives. Sadly, I did not respond in repentance at that time; as a result, Jeff and I left Northland in 1991 and the spiritual quality of our lives and marriage began to plummet. Thankfully, the power of God's Word and the conviction of the Holy Spirit continued to work until I came to the place of brokenness in 1993.

God now had my heart, and I responded in obedience to him. This meant I needed to make things right with those I had hurt, specifically my husband and children. My husband's life, however, only got worse, and one year later (1994) he ended his life. Having two children, who were seven and five, and being pregnant with our third, I decided after much prayer to return to Northland after the birth of my child. Over the next sixteen years, God continued his life-changing work in my heart and gave me the privilege of teaching.

My thoughts were filled with memories of Northland as I continued on my walk. What if Jeff and I had stayed? Would our lives have played out differently? Why didn't I respond to God's conviction earlier? Why was I so stubborn and foolish? If only I hadn't been such a contentious wife ... perhaps my husband would not have fallen. The questions went on and on. My heart was broken over the many foolish choices I made during my first seven years of marriage, choices that have deeply scarred my children. The sadness was intense.

Then I remembered the wonderful words of Psalm 130:

> If You, LORD, should mark iniquities,
> O Lord, who could stand?
> But there is forgiveness with You,
> That You may be feared.
>
> (vv. 3–4)

Oh, how marvelous is God's forgiveness! I was also reminded of Psalm 103:

> He has not dealt with us according to
>   our sins,
> Nor punished us according to
>   our iniquities.
> For as the heavens are high above the earth,
> So great is His mercy toward those who
>   fear Him.
>
> (vv. 10–11)

Oh, how great is God's mercy! I thought of the apostle Paul, who said that God's grace was "exceedingly abundant" to him. Prior to his conversion, he was "a blasphemer, a persecutor, and an insolent man" (1 Timothy 1:12–14). I too have experienced the matchless grace of God.

My sadness now turned to joy and heartfelt praise. God had turned ashes into beauty and had given me the garment of praise to replace the spirit of heaviness (Isaiah 61:3). I don't need to live in the past, and I must not dwell on things I have no ability to change. Yes, I experience much heartache from those wrong choices, and the emotional pain can be and often is excruciating, but the story doesn't end there. My prayer has become that of the psalmist:

> Oh, send out Your light and Your truth!

> Let them lead me;
> Let them bring me to Your holy hill
> And to Your tabernacle.
> Then I will go to the altar of God,
> To God my exceeding joy.
>
> *(Psalm 43:3–4)*

God *is* my exceeding joy! He has done great things. He is infinitely bigger than any struggle we may face—and yes, he is even able to use our mistakes. This, of course, is not an excuse for our wrong choices. We will reap what we sow, but as we choose to surrender to God's agenda, we will experience his wonderful grace, mercy, and forgiveness. He never wastes any experience or pain.

We can and must choose the path of joy over depression. Let God give you a ministry through your sorrow as you surrender to his purpose, responding with humility and obedience. What will be the result? God will give you a life message that will impact the multitudes. You will be able to minister to hurting people in a way you never thought possible (see 2 Corinthians 1:3–7).

I am continually amazed at the opportunities God gives me to minister to those filled with sadness. I have boxes full of letters from many who have expressed thanks for God's work in their lives. These letters are both humbling and encouraging, as women share how God has used the testimony of his grace in my life to give them hope.

Women often ask me if giving my testimony is still hard. My answer is always the same: yes. But life is not about me or even my pain; it is all about God. He has called me to this ministry of giving hope to hurting women, and I wholeheartedly embrace it. Embracing his ministry is my prayer for you as well.

> Now may the God of hope fill you with
> all joy and peace in believing, that you
> may abound in hope by the power of the
> Holy Spirit.
>
> (Romans 15:13)

Personal Application Projects

Chapter 1

1. Read Judges 10:6–16; Jonah 4:2; Nahum 1:2–7;
   John 2:14–17.

   (a) List several different emotions our Lord
       experiences.

   (b) Do any of these emotions surprise you?
       Why or why not?

2. Read Daniel 9:3–19.

   (a) If God was holy, just, and righteous, but
       not merciful, gracious, or forgiving, what
       would be the consequences for our lives?

   (b) What if the opposite was true? What
       if God was merciful, gracious, and
       forgiving, but not holy, just, and
       righteous? How would this affect our
       lives?

   (c) What did Daniel understand about the

character of God that he expressed in
this marvelous prayer?

3. Read Mark 5. This chapter introduces us to
three people who experienced great sorrow
because of difficult circumstances (demon
possession, disease, and death).

   (a) Which character qualities did the
   Lord Jesus reveal as he dealt with each
   individual?

   (b) How did Jesus turn their sorrow into joy?

   (c) In what ways could they have used their
   sorrow as a ministry to others (especially
   see vv. 19–20)?

4. Read 2 Corinthians 1:3–7. What did the
apostle Paul teach us about the ministry
of sorrow?

5. Consider the circumstances depressing you.
Ask yourself how you can turn them into a
ministry to others.

Chapter 2

1. Read Ezra 9:1–3; Nehemiah 1:4; 2:1–2. Both Ezra and Nehemiah received distressing news. In what physical and emotional ways did they respond?

2. Suffering and its related sorrow are designed to mold us into the image of Christ. Read Hebrews 2:9–10, 14–18; 4:15–16; 5:7–8.

   (a) What were some of the emotions Jesus experienced (5:7–8)?

   (b) According to these verses, what are some of the reasons or purposes behind the suffering Jesus experienced?

3. Read James 1:2–4 and Romans 5:3–5. What do these verses reveal about God's goal in our suffering and sorrow?

4. Read Ezra 9:4–15 and Nehemiah 1:5–11. How did Ezra and Nehemiah's view of God affect their interpretation of their distressing circumstances?

5. How does your view of God affect the way you interpret the distressing circumstances contributing to your depression?

Chapter 3

1. Read 1 Peter 2:19–21, 23. What do these verses reveal about how we should respond to difficult circumstances that bring sorrow?

2. Read Romans 12:14–21 and 1 Peter 3:9, 14, 17.

    (a) How should we respond to difficult people?

    (b) Instead of choosing to be depressed when people mistreat us, what should our attitude be, according to these verses?

3. Read 1 Peter 5:6–7.

    (a) How should we respond to God when he brings difficulty into our lives?

    (b) What specific steps did the apostle Peter instruct us to follow in these verses?

4. How do you respond to difficult circumstances and people? Are you depressed, or are you humbling yourself before God and overcoming evil with good?

Chapter 4

1. Read 1 Peter 1:3–9. What promises did Peter say belong to the child of God and should motivate him or her to embrace difficulty with joy?

2. Read 1 Peter 4:12–13. According to these verses, we can respond with joy in the midst of trials. How is that possible?

3. Read 1 Thessalonians 4:13–18. What truths did Paul teach in these verses that enable us to sorrow but not as those without hope?

4. Read 1 Peter 5:10. What is God's promise to us regarding suffering?

5. In light of these truths, does the believer have any reason to live in a state of depression?

Where Can I Get More Help?

Berg, Jim, *Changed into His Image: God's Plan for Transforming Your Life* (Greenville, SC: BJU Press, 1999)

DeMoss, Nancy Leigh, *Choosing Gratitude* (Chicago: Moody, 2009)

Elliot, Elisabeth, *A Path through Suffering: Discovering the Relationship between God's Mercy and Our Pain* (Ann Arbor, MI: Vine, 1992)

——*Keep a Quiet Heart* (Ann Arbor, MI: Vine, 1995)

Peace, Martha, *Damsels in Distress: Biblical Solutions for Problems Women Face* (Phillipsburg, NJ: P&R, 2006)

Smith, M.D., Robert, *The Christian Counselor's Medical Desk Reference* (Stanley, NC: Timeless Texts, 2000)

Tada, Joni Eareckson, *31 Days toward Intimacy with God* (Colorado Springs: Multnomah, 2005)

Welch, Edward T., *Blame It on the Brain? Distinguishing Chemical Imbalances, Brain Disorders, and Disobedience* (Phillipsburg, NJ: P&R, 1998)

——*Depression: A Stubborn Darkness* (Winston-Salem, NC: Punch Press, 2004)

Carol Trahan Ministries at www.caroltrahanministries.org includes CD messages and articles for women who suffer

END NOTES

1 "Depressed," at Dictionary.com, http://dictionary.reference.com/browse/depressed; accessed June 3, 2011.

2 One helpful resource, among others, is Robert Smith, M.D., The Christian Counselor's Medical Desk Reference (Stanley, NC: Timeless Texts, 2000).

3 Quoted in Warren Wiersbe, The Best of A. W. Tozer (Harrisburg, PA: Christian Publications, 1978), 120.

4 Mrs. Charles Cowman, Streams in the Desert (Grand Rapids: Zondervan, 1996), 213–214.

5 John MacArthur, The MacArthur Study Bible (Nashville: Word Publishing, 1997), 1511.

BOOKS IN THE HELP! SERIES INCLUDE...

(More titles in preparation)